In
Any
of
These
Towns

poems

Stephanie Kendrick

In Any of These Towns © Stephanie Kendrick, 2022
Cover Art © iStock: bobmadbob, 2022
Author Photo © Stephanie Kendrick, 2022

ISBN: 979-8-9855242-5-3

Sheila-Na-Gig Editions
Russell, KY
Hayley Mitchell Haugen, Editor
www.sheilanagigblog.com

Acknowledgments:

Anti-Heroin Chic: "Solstice Steals Their Bones, Turns Them to Snow," "En Route to Family Christmas," "Below the Surface"

Gyroscope Review: "An Ode to Kids Who Pluck Flowers From Trashcans," "When Beth Texts to Ask for Money the Day After Bezos Flies Toward Space"

I Thought I Heard a Cardinal Sing: "Mammaw Comes Back a Cardinal," "Closed Road Ahead"

Lunch Bucket Brigade: "At the Thursday Night Community Dinner," "My Husband and I Drive Through Our Hometown for the First Time in Years," "Proletarian Girl in Black," "When the City Closes the Firehouse"

Main Street Rag: "In Any of These Towns"

Northern Appalachia Review: "Transcendence," "What is Left Behind"

Pudding Magazine: "The Townspeople Say They Are Stuck," "Florida Has Gone to Her Head"

Red Fez: "Apartment Complex"

Still: The Journal: "Mad women," "Right at Home"

Verse Virtual: "Puppets"

For all the people who kept me afloat, and the places
that couldn't pull me under.

Contents

I.

II.

III.

I.

Amends

There are people in this town
who have kicked gravel onto neighbors' lawns,
revved engines before 7am,
carved initials into sidewalks, letters
that don't belong together now.

A man sits on his porch, smokes non-filters,
exhales slurs at the boys with long hair,
the girls who don't let him close enough,
and the ones who did.

A stray dog sits at his feet—tail tucked,
tips of ears resting on the cold porch.
She doesn't move at the morsels of words
that fall from his chin, doesn't know intent
of *mangy bitch* or *smelly old hound*—

There are people in this town
who tell their stories only in a secret language,
hide from those who might know,
whisper them over and over again, praying
no one ever finds them.

At the Thursday Night Community Dinner

kids with Kool-Aid lips and spaghetti-stain collars
sit in circles to mock town bylaws, fine-tune
the syllables of a secret language of change
away from waxing-moon ears of grownups.

Never a crumb left at the end of the night,
but the children sneak morsels of hope.
Even though tomorrow brings more hunger,
tonight they dream.

This is how it happens, the creation of Gods—
desperate to quiet their own hollowed selves
they plant seeds and forge paths for the growth.

In sleep they call to one another
with secret words, plan demolitions
to make room for goat farms,
fields of echinacea and wild berries.

Here, grandmothers move out
and mothers come back home.
They teach them to listen
for the seal-pop of mason jars,

learn all the ways to trap moments
and keep them sweet.

Eviction

When wind blows white ashes
from rubble where a house once stood,
we are left with scraps from the burn—

frames and furniture, bits of bone
and stained glass. Neighbors gather in prayer,
wait in line for confession, to claw

their way out of the remains—
stagnant smoke below uncaged birds.

Angels tighten their masks
and strain to hear.

Slinging Bible Verses and Pepperoni Rolls

For God so loved the world he gave
the village kids pepperoni rolls for a quarter
if they could show the baker a sticker
they got for reciting verse at First Baptist.

And isn't it something, to a nine-year-old
to stand in the pulpit of the very first Baptist church
on this great big Earth until the nine-year-old
is a twenty-something and finds out

that there are First Baptists everywhere
and the Earth is a lot smaller
and maybe less loved than John said.

And after whispering Luke over and over
until their tongues blistered,
Blessed are you who are poor

they still knew nothing of kingdoms
of Heaven that weren't adorned
with repo notices, and crumpled aluminum

that covered those warm pepperoni rolls.
Matthew might have called them cannibals.
Take this, eat my body, they'd joke,

but this wasn't *daily bread*
and hunger isn't a metaphor

so on Wednesday nights they repeated
the words of men they'd never known
until those words were all they could hear,
over the rumbling in their bellies.

Solstice Steals Their Bones,
Turns Them to Snow

First it was Mammaw, piano chained
to her back so she'd carry it with her
to Heaven. She said she would play it
to whichever God met her at the gate
ready to kiss the arthritis from her
fingers, put the pain back into her spine
where it belonged. The doctors offered
her a halo when she was thirteen
and she wore it everywhere,
never mind the screws in her temple,
she sang hymns and fancied herself Jesus.

Then corner-store Jo, with wind that shifted
the hips of blue grass and whistled
through our ears, taught us the taste of twang
and the ache that comes with being off-
key even after all the music had stopped.
Fans flooded the local paper with memories,
a river of ink spilled to scrawl every way his sound
still moved through masses, tickled ears
of his widows, curled the tongues
of all of us, mouthing every word he ever sang.

Now, Pastor Pete wheezes ballads of Yukon,
the time the temperature fell
to 80 below. As locals stepped outside,
their breath hissed as it froze, turned to dust
midair before falling to the ground.
When he says he'd like to travel North
to die, he really means he wants his breath
to turn to music again, force it from his lungs,
make it shout in the air, so that when
the neighbors jump from their skins,
he can say it was his voice
that moved them.

When Children in This Town Turn to Seed

You can tell when you see an empty-handed mother
wandering through the baking aisle over and over
sometimes picking up a sack of flour, sometimes
checking the paper for holes, scanning each corner

of the bag with sorried eyes to see where the white
falls from, setting the bag back on the shelf, sifting
the feral powder through wire fingers so it falls
on her toes like snow that could stun a morning dew,

thawing herself again and again with each step. You
can watch her do this several times, watch her kill
an hour folding herself through shoppers who need
sugars and oils, and those who don't stop long enough

to check for holes. She remembers a birthday,
the way her son's eyes closed to blow out candles,
careful not to reveal his wish because she taught him
wishes must be kept secret to stand a chance.

She remembers the paraffin smoke, how
when he opened his eyes, he saw the way it danced
around the rays of light; he asked her where it goes.
You can tell when you see her bend a scorched knee

until eye-level with the salt, watch her turn the cap
to open holes, raise the shaker to parted lips, tip it
until all she tastes is someone else's tears—her mouth
a wound refusing to heal; he asked her where it goes.

You can tell when you see an empty-handed mother,
eyes silent as roots, reaching as if she were buried,
tucked at the bottom of a hole, yearning to spread
and find the light, so she can answer where it goes.

Kids' Night

As in any other diner in a dead-end town
children cram quarters in a rusty jukebox,
hop-scotch between the tables,

careful to land *only* on the cracks,
their bare and callused feet,
careless of their mothers' backs.

This is their night.
Mom and Dad stay home to lukewarm nightly news
and burn their tongues on boiling tea.

Tonight, kids cup their tiny palms and scoop
filthy hands into tubs of soft serve, hardened
by a stronger kind of cold.

They thaw it between their fingers, smear
the cream against their bellies, howl
at a flickering neon light that has advertised Coke

to them since they were babies.
They grin at one another with hollowed mouths,
pull what broken shards are left from behind

their lips, smash the pieces underneath their heels,
until every bit of everything
crumbles and blows away.

A Birth

Gravel gathers in the mouths of mothers
so that *get out* sounds like *eat this*,

and when casseroles are exchanged,
everyone prays for poison.

Babies lip lazily at droplets of nectar that weep
from the chests and temples and spines of fathers,

the first tingle of tongue tricks them toward silence.

This is how the statues are carved—
fists form to chisel frowns and drill holes
where eyes are supposed to be.

Women spit tears at the stone feet,
mutter curses at pills and poverty and gravity—

everything that pulls them back.

When the City Closes the Firehouse

First they fool you into thinking
flames are a thing of the past,
so that when your nose tickles with
aldehyde aromas, you dismiss this—

a distant memory too blurry to see,
but close enough to give you shivers.

Overnight the mural on the side
of what used to be a barber shop
fades into disarray—
the two-dimensional church steps
chip away, the old coal locomotive
derails from a track that crumbles
with the rest of the foundation.
The city park disappears under ivy.

Feral cats screech ordinances at dawn,
daring those who are left to abstain.

Then the ground absorbs sidewalks,
and there is someone to thank
for these feet that understand terrain
tortured by the frantic hollowing
of moles, but you have never seen that
someone, and they didn't give *us*
the good sense to dig our way out.

Now you are left among the rubble, one
hand grips a jug of gasoline, the other
covers your own eyes.

These flames are your blood,
this smoke, your breath—
lifting this city to the clouds.

An Ode to Kids
Who Pluck Flowers From Trashcans

There were no signs at the cemetery
that told you not to take the plastic
faded flowers from the trash,
to resurrect the polyester Primulas
from a grave smattered with Pepsi cans
and remnants from a beater's ashtray.
Even if there were, what business
does a silken rose have to finish
its usefulness soaked in Fireball,
salty tissue, abandoned Bible verses?
To beautify was born inside you,
awake and waiting to take hold
of your mother's lonely shoulders,
a boy at the playground bleeding
from his knee, or these graying gravesites,
barely brightened under sun.
No one told you
color stays buried with some,
while the rest lay adorned and vibrant
even as they rot; yes, no one ever says
that decomposing is beauty
in motion, so we trap it in a box,
cover it with dirt.
You don't miss a beat.
The *click click click* of a bicycle chain,
it is you, sent here to show
the rest of us how to question
what we toss aside.
And even when they hang the sign,
DO NOT TAKE
FLOWERS FROM TRASH
I will cling to my faith,
that those words mean nothing
to the only ones who question
how we can bury lives so precious
and every time forget the seeds.

The Townspeople Say They Are Stuck

The city forgot to lay pavement here.
Angels tiptoe through the gravel,
careful not to kick up dust or part
the limestone. In March, street signs
vanished, turned to flood, evaporated to ash.
Children buried their hands in the piles,
tossed it in the air and danced in their confetti.
Jill from the grant committee lost her pen,
found a vacuum in the rubble to erase
their party. By May, she forged a trail.
The shelves in the corner store emptied
faster than Jill's decanter, and her path grew
crowded—stories of women trampled by boots.
By July, the stench was so bad that no one walked
the path where pavement should have been. Gnats
circled bones that held tight to tendon, children
studied horticulture, and elders felt strong regret
about their degrees in accounting or French.
On Wednesday, the town gathered at council,
widowers in boots with lists of demands. Mayor,
eyes swollen, truck still full of gas, declared
Jill resigned from her position on the grant committee.
Any and all questions shall be directed at her
sinew-stitched bones scattered
on the trail she forged in Spring.
The gnats dispersed.
The widowers bowed their heads
and wandered away, until
the children showed up,
requesting seeds.

Puppets

Our children gather in the square
for the spectacle. Hunters
lift their trophy skins,
turn them inside out and back again.

Councilmen slide their crocodile hands
into the furs, forefingers move
the tiny mouths that hid
cheekfuls of acorns hours before.

During squirrel season in the village,
we gather what we can—
creature, nut, or fallen apples
haloed by hungry flies.

We hollow the insides,
pluck from shell,
peel skin from meat,
leave the bones behind.

After the show, jaws sore from laughter,
our children plot the hollowing
of the Councilmen, wonder
if their tiny hands are large enough
to move their mouths.

II.

JoJo Throws House Parties to the People Like Loaves of Bread

We line up early, stomachs churning
for any vibration to shift our hips,
flip our hair to Heaven, raise hands
in fists to purge prayer from palms.

He stands on the lawn at the gate, glazed
snowflake eyes twinkle the closer we get.
One by one he ushers us in, lures us
with the promise of skin and sweat.

The floor in front of the stage floats filthy
under bare feet stomping melody holes
into the original pine. Pieces splinter
but we can't feel the pierced callus

over the beating bass, the electricity
between bones, tongues flicking verse against teeth—
everyone is here to kneel and be saved
by shirtless mustache man at the microphone.

We destroy his home and forget the ways
to ask forgiveness. When the music stops,
we die all over again—turn back to quiet
cubicle keyboard ringtone harmony hymns,

spines hungry for next Saturday night.

Mad women

look all the way to the fingertips, abused
by our own mouths. So many people
are the tips of our fingers, chewed raw
until it hurts to hold anything.

We are the palms of outstretched hands.
How many women can fit here, balanced
on lines that stretch from knuckle to wrist?

We are dew drops on a gum tree leaf.
Can you see your smile in here?
See the way we move so we won't
disrupt our surface tension.
So many people, these reflections,
staying so still, trying not to burst.

Look again at the fingertips, rough edges
callused to the core. So many people
are the hardened skin of our hands, stripped bare

only to heal again and again until nothing else
gets through. We are fists of overflowing arms.
How many of you have felt this heat,
synapse sparks that spew like lava from your mouth?

We are the spikes on a honey locust.
Can you find a way to hold us, anyway?
Sharp and ready, we wait for unsuspected touch,
blanket the ground with the leaves that fall around us.

We share these parts of ourselves with you,
beg you to rip them out, smile
as you carry them away.

At the Tanning Salon

Becky keeps her beds hot and lights dim
for spicy girls and ice-cold women, messy
buns or stilettos, sweatpants and chewing tobacco,
all with their own way of staining their chests.

She keeps a TV humming in the lobby,
weather channel on loop. And every time
someone asks why the west-coast-weather
in an east-coast-shop, Becky says, *Don't*
look to strangers for answers you already know.

On Wednesdays when the village tests the sirens,
she hits the mute button and stands on top of her desk,
wails until the LEDs tremble in every room—
It is never only a test! It is only ever a test.

She sweet-talks children who wait for mothers,
converts them with questions that leave a mark.
Little mouths wide open, ears pried apart,
perfect frail visionaries—
she warns them of their own tongues.

She sweats conspiracies and captures them
in Juicy Fruit bubbles she pops behind her lips,
will not hear that she didn't get it right, melts
those words in her palms until there's nothing—

nothing left to do but layer them on top of skin,
wait for the heat to do its work.

Copper Heart

Jenny has kaleidoscope legs,
stomps on my heart in every shade.
Color seeps from her body
and always leaves a stain.

Jenny has a bottleneck brain,
draws me in unwittingly,
confuses me with signaled hips
and signs that do not let me out.

Jenny has a woodgrain pout.
Tested for termites,
and full of nails, don't trust
the holey patches.

Jenny has guitar-string eyelashes.
From every flutter comes a sound
that renders me tone-deaf and dizzy.
I want to pluck them apart, but

Jenny has a copper heart.
Every so often she tries to clean it
with salt-soak and vinegar tears.

She can't get that thing shiny no more.
Jenny has feet welded to the floor.

Florida Has Gone to Her Head

Discount tobacco and tourist hips,
Spanglish stitched in her tongue
with her mother's rainbow thread.

Swollen lips from sweat-slicked 6-packs,
Everglade fire ants she pulls from swamps,
anything to still feel a sting in her bed.

Sidewalk grouper and mango mash
she can't go hungry
when she's never really been fed.

Mosquitos and Miami sucked her dry.
All the mouths of each have left her
quite insane and stuffed with dread.

Welcome mat flipped upside down,
faded prayer flag on the doublewide
keeping doors locked from the dead.

Florida has gone to her head.

Iris the Dog Warden

She strolls the streets of her village,
armed with bones and mace,

picks fleas from her socks, squeezes
bodies with fingertips she lifts to her lips.

She saves the blood,
lets strays lap it from her hands—

From room to empty room she saunters
on all fours, sniffs the carpet, salivates

at the hint of stranger smells.
She finds those who wander from their home,

all skin and bone and whimper,
the ones whose kisses turn to growls.

She nips at the necks of those who pet her
before she gets used to their scent.

She licks the wounds
before they know,

does not wait for the moon
to howl.

Crazy Patty

makes her signs in the mornings,
torn cardboard and stolen Sharpies—
warnings of doom her neighbors do not see.
She cannot waste time
on chem trails and pharmaceuticals
when there are things here
worth running from.

Her mother was never the same
after the CAT scan, never said *love*
after the headaches started,
never trusted vegetables after the infidelity,
and superstitiously sprinkled dirt
in all of Patty's pockets.

Now Patty sips boiled water and shouts
at kids walking home from school, teaches
syllables like *indoctrination* and *lucid,*
grins when they try to teach her
freak show and *insane*

as if those words weren't hammered
into her when she herself was learning
to write inside the lines.

At dinner she leaves her sign at her post,
limps home barefoot on perfectly fine legs,
ponders tomorrow's enlightenment of the masses,
pockets full of seeds.

Proletarian Girl in Black

You know the type.
She exits the womb with callused
palms, brow wrinkled
with wisdom beat into her bones
before her mother was even conceived.
Watch her wake before the alarm,
siphon coffee from her own pores,
dress in charlatan contempt,
shave the hair from her scalp.

Marvel as she crumbles to ash.
Beg her to stop.

Mammaw Comes Back a Cardinal

She visits at the window
while I wash dishes,
my hands as wrinkled as hers
before she grew into her wings.
This is the longest
we've been together
without *Days of Our Lives*,
or other scripted sermons
filling the silence
of the decades between us.
She is still as gray, and sings
her own songs of faith
that entice even the worms
that have burrowed deepest.
I still can't land the harmony,
but try to find the pitch,
even now, knowing full well
those songs were never meant for me.

She is the Statue in the Center of Town

Hers is a shoulder where you can lay your head,
rest your ear on lumps of knotted flesh, hold
back the weight of dreams. She wants your face
to absorb the heat of her breath while she shares
her secrets with you. This will not last,

her thighs relaxed, her pulse rhythmic. Still
she suspends time, and can't you see her eyes
burn memory into yours? Don't you hear the voice
in your head disappear into steam from her
lips? Close your mouth and claw your way

to her hips. Grip them tight with ancestral hands,
pull apart until the bones shatter, and open
your eyes. This is where the world begins.

Transcendence

The road to my mother's home could lead anywhere.
Trees that rest heavy on power lines could be any
trees, and the sky, today void of clouds, could suffocate

any of us. Things are happening this year, bending
on top of strings not made to hold our dead,
like webs I sweep from the corners of my porch.

The news notes those who have left us,
tally-mark reminders of impermanence that we chase
with double bourbons and lethal amounts of blue

light that we cannot soak in fast enough. We dream
about tomorrows that already happened. She starts
a pot of coffee, another leaf surrenders to the ground.

Trapped

There is death in the walls of this home.   I smell it,
the smell of vanishing. Not quite
soured milk or meat gone gray and seepy.   Not quite
parsley forgotten or wet shoes   forgotten
or sheets forgotten in the wash.   Not quite
the way I remember the way   you
lingered in the mattress, after
the fevers and shakes   not quite
a puddle almost all the way   gone.

I sniff the corners of the rooms of   this body
rip out strips of carpet, but once
I have been washed in it, I   cannot
find the source of its emptiness,   cannot
trace the reversal, every inch of skin,
every inch of drywall, every memory
soaked in the rot of every part
I have tried so hard to   forget.

34

Billy at the Depot

Billy waits, cross-legged with a smile,
waves at women who push strollers,
gives bits of his sandwich to squirrels
who have learned to trust his palm.

Hours float in air like dust,
a man sets foot on the tracks to cross
to the other side. Billy runs to the man,
decks him so hard, square in the jaw,

so he flies backwards, lands
right on his ass. I saw this happen,
heard only the sound of fist to flesh,

a mother's flattened hand meeting the fat
of a rump roast, a belly's accidental landing
on the surface of water, a bird slapping
against the window of a moving car.

He mutters something about "my old lady,"
muffled by his mustache and the blood
dripping from his knuckles.

He doesn't see me, doesn't hear
the excited beating of my heart.

One Creation Story

His hands, ivory, and slick as bone, cold against my skin
pull uneasy laughs from my lips.

Years ago, when I found that dog, she was free—
leash around her neck and nothing else.

Free: *adjective*, no longer confined.
Free: *adjective*, given or available without charge.

This is how it works. Poetry, I mean.
In the crease of the bend of my knee, where his fingertips

meet the flesh during full-palmed tickle of my leg—
A half-moon scar remains, does not retreat at the sight of sun.

Canine: *noun*, a dog.
Canine: *noun*, a pointed tooth.

Yes. This is how it works. His hands, marble slabs
pin my knees down. I tried so hard

to find this lost dog's home. Knocked on every stranger's door.
She licked at my feet, kept pace with me

until we found her rightful home.
A lonely tree, other half of leash.

Abandon: *verb*, to give up someone.
Abandon: *noun*, complete lack of restraint.

Don't you see yet, how it works?

Standing Nude With Spread Legs and Yellow Shawl

The words come from her eyes—
Name me Martha.

Martha with the yellow shawl,
mustard-stained madness hides
the tangles in her hair.

Don't you see she's telling you
to pluck a tendril from behind her ear,
softly lead it through the eye,

sew shut the hole that stares from her chest?
First, crawl inside.

Don't you know the sound
of waiting?

When Beth Texts to Ask for Money
the Day After Bezos Flies Toward Space

She tossed me a pack of menthols,
taught me to drag slow, exhale cool.
Stargazers on the creaking wood, we talked
through the entire pack, stories of girls

full of dirt and gravel, everything
heavy enough to keep us
grounded to the Earth.

I haven't seen her in fifteen years,
cross-legged on the dock as the sun set,
snakes slithering on the surface
around a scattered reflection of the moon.

Tonight, different moon, familiar story—
No one told her she is star dust,
so she stayed,
siphoned herself until nothing was left
but empty space.

I tell her a story, too,
that I just don't have the cash right now.
And for a minute, I am every bit Bezos,
soaring far and away from her

and everyone else I love,
who can't outrun the gravity.

A Funeral

Earth softens today to make room
for rest—a womb of dirt.

This town is held up by bones of mothers,
its border sinew-stitched to hold us in.

Inside, lips of wool grass
slick with dew
open under sighs of breeze
welcoming them back.

III.

In Any of Ourselves

I have eased my way inside a person.
Silent and coy, invited even—
open mouths,
fingertips to face,
a deep inhale.

I have found ways to bind
to parts of those
who weren't the wiser.
I've left bits of me behind
in scattered breath,
the richness of blood,
a trickle of tears.

I have sometimes only
invaded long enough
to create myself,
again
and again,
and again,
even after the destruction
has left me
weak.

What is Left Behind

The shelves are empty again, picked clean
like sinew stripped from bone, nothing left
but marrow and dust.
We cough pleas
into wind, pray they land in mouths
of strangers who recognize the taste
of hope and desperation.
We cough joy
into fists, unable to peel our fingers
from palm, the soft tips warmed
against callus and pulse.
We cough whispers
into the ears of our mothers, hope they fit snug
and turn to screams,
so the lullabies they gave
us never leave them.
We cough inheritance
into lessons we teach our children,
promise them we are different, teach them
that they are different.
We cough memory
into masks that block breath from escaping,
inhale to taste one last time the recipes
from our childhood table.
We cough splintered words
through head and heart. They shatter
like bone, the only pieces
we can attach ourselves to.

My Husband and I Drive Through Our Hometown for the First Time in Years

The graffiti on the door of Dixon's Hardware, now defunct,
is supposed to be a swastika, but as it turned out, the artist
does not know how to paint a swastika, and so we talk
of intent and what other artists are just idiots who got it right.

He used red, the color of Hitler's telephone, so we talk
about whether he knew this, and why I assume the artist is a he,
and this might be a metaphor for speaking through bloodshed,
but my husband says it was likely the only color he had.

When I was ten, old man Dixon used the N word
in a joke he told my mom when all she asked was *where can I find
a socket wrench*? They laughed, and I felt something in my belly
I didn't have a word for, and I made myself throw up that day.

Before we cross the corporation limit, I look back so I'll recall
the direction the lines are painted; that way when I tell the story
I have an extra detail. I notice fresh blooms on dogwood trees,
and know the only things we can use are what we have at the time.

En Route to a Family Christmas

Every year we pass the same schoolhouse,
the one that never had indoor plumbing,
never felt the quake of fluid rushing
behind its walls, or under its parquet tiles.

I confess to him, it's the one I'd park behind,
under moons because no one could see me
from the road, and there's something romantic
about hiding, and about a moonlit schoolhouse.

He wasn't one of them, in the passenger seat
of my '95 Mustang, so I'm careful to leave out
the memorable details—a palm stained
with motor oil, a mustache sweet with nicotine.

He has some stories too: a covered bridge off 56
that can't bear the weight of anything anymore.
We pass it two miles from the schoolhouse.
He inhales and holds it. I try not to wonder

what she smelled like, how his hands warmed
inside her thighs, how their lips emulsified, or
if that mustache still smells of menthol.

And just like every year before, as we pass
the covered bridge I take his hand,
bring it to my lips as we both exhale.

This Town

Everyone in this town is a monster.
Even the shy ones howl at night
into the thick of their bed pillow.

Everyone in this town dies harder
than their neighbors, prescriptions hang
like silver chains near lilac hearts.

Everyone's hero is the pharmacist.
She reads and fills and reads and fills,
adds a little extra for those she likes.

Everyone in this town is someone else.
Names drift away with wind, disguises
show up in little orange plastic bottles.

Everyone's kids sling unmarked pills at the park,
smoke hand-rolled cigarettes, save
tobacco bits under their nails for later.

Everyone in this town is too early
and does not know when to leave.
They always stay past their welcome.

Everyone in this town is hungry.
Breadcrumb trails are gobbled up.
Mouths hover above starved bellies—
cannot stay still—
they have no place to go.

Closed Road Ahead

The road is crumbling in the center
of town, promises of a sinkhole
elate the children, propel them
to chatter of the center of Earth,
mysteries that widen their eyes—
tiny, globed galaxies light-years away.
They have always been warned
stars sting to the touch, all we are
was already in space anyway. So
they race to the center of town
and dance
in the soup-bowl asphalt, hungry
for everything in the whole world
to prove to everyone else
that even down here
is just as empty,
and just as vast.

Apartment Complex

Cubes of rooms and walls and chatter
separated by locked doors and numbers,

rumors of who is taking the car stereos,
leaving faceplates scattered in the lot—

plastic confetti leftover from desperate
Saturdays. We all know

who breaks into the laundry room. We warn
the others to guard the machines, wait

for final tumble, for every drop to sizzle dry.
The dumpster stays stuffed with neglect,

items left for dead, like the shriveled ficus
abandoned with Fireball bottles and sweaters

full of cigarette holes. Miss Leah from 435
crawls inside and saves

any filthy thing worth a resurrection,
hauls it limp back to her room and whispers life

back into its cracks. She offers a swig of beer
to the skinny kid who steals cable from neighbors,

giggles when he flips her the bird and runs away,
leaving the wire dangling from the box,

all of us that wire, ready to shock anyone
who will offer us their hand.

Right at Home

Inside an olive-green house on coal ridge
everything dies and floats as ash
like dust the train kicks up and delivers.

Inside you might hold your breath
unless you love the way stale cigar smoke
flows through sinus trails and hides

inside your chest. Here is where it lingers,
the sound of tracks trembling, the smell
of something always about to burn.

Inside each room footprints scale the walls,
fade before they reach the ceiling. Listen
to the spirit fists pounding to escape.

Inside your own fists, the vibration
of knuckle and palm, the white noise
that helped you sleep until morning. Listen

inside the back of your own throat, the screams
you gulped down, locked away in your own attic
inside that olive-green house on coal ridge.

Below the Surface

Sometimes the river looks this way,
rushes west as though there's still gold
to discover, as if teenagers who skinny dip
inside her are blood-thirsty like bats,
soaking their claws in her mouth, then
pulling them out before the leeches take hold.

Sometimes the river slows enough to reflect
their faces like my grandfather's Buick
as it coasts to full stop in his garage.
He takes a peppermint from his suit,
twists away the plastic and
convinces his mouth it is not menthol.

Sometimes the river stops completely,
forced frozen by a February breeze;
my sisters, driven mad by living underwater,
scratch the surface and learn
to breathe with closed mouths,
learn to swim with fists —

yes, sometimes,
the river looks like this.

In Sedalia

No one picks the pawpaws —
a curious trait for a village
so starved. They fall

and rot, because even the squirrels
won't take the charity.
Flies pick at mush that oozes through

bruised and sallow skin, spit the sugar out
at the children dusted with railroad soot
and mothers' afternoon exasperation.

These trees have taken over
between Sam's gym and what will be
a boutique, or brewery if Jill gets the grant.

Each tree has twenty pawpaw bunches
scattered under cabana leaves,
sending sweet promises to visitors,

through the nose, each whiff a whisper,
a beckoning.

Almost no one knows the names of streets,
but they can tell a stranger all the ways
to get the hell out.

That way,

past the crumbled building
with the bruised-up eyes and busted lip,
don't stop

until you lose the smell
of metallic mango and dirt,
hurry!

before these roots take hold.

In Any of These Towns

On any given day,
one might stumble upon
a field of dead bodies.

You might spend an entire life,
looking at them from a passenger side window,
all polyester flowers and a smattering of flags.

Then one day, you walk out the automatic doors
at your local grocer, each arm hugging a bag
of fruit you swear you won't let rot this time,

and you see it across the street:
a garden commissioned by the city.

The seeds are people,
and they have sprouted into stone,
begging you
to remember their names.

Stephanie Kendrick is the author of *Places We Feel Warm* (Main Street Rag Publishing, 2021), editor of "Periodical Poetry." With a Masters of Social Sciences from Ohio University, she is the Major Unusual Incident Compliance Coordinator at the Athens County Board of Developmental Disabilities. She serves as a Village Councilwoman in Albany, Ohio, where she lives with her phenomenal husband and their talented son. On any given day, you might find her binging on trash TV, hiking through the hills of Athens, or training jiu-jitsu. Her poems have appeared in *Sheila-Na-Gig online*, *Gyroscope Review*, *Northern Appalachia Review*, *Poets Reading the News*, *Still: The Journal*, and elsewhere. Visit her website to check out more of her work, and upcoming events at stephthepoet.org.

Sheila-Na-Gig Editions

CPSIA information can be obtained
at www.ICGtesting.com
Printed in the USA
JSHW030304070123
35608JS00003B/115